D0163870

Eighteenth-Century Imitative Counterpoint

MUSIC FOR ANALYSIS

Heterick Memorial Library
Ohio Northern University
Ada, Ohio 45810

WALLACE BERRY

EDWARD CHUDACOFF

The University of Michigan

Eighteenth-Century Imitative Counterpoint

MUSIC FOR ANALYSIS

PRENTICE-HALL, INC., Englewood Cliffs, New Jersey

TO THE MEMORY OF

Dr. Hans T. David

©1969
by PRENTICE-HALL, Inc.,
Englewood Cliffs, New Jersey

All rights reserved. No part of this book
may be reproduced in any form or by any means,
without permission in writing from the publisher.

Printed in the United States of America

ISBN: 0-13-246843-3

Library of Congress Catalog Card Number: 75-76230

10 9 8 7 6 5 4 3 2 1

PRENTICE-HALL INTERNATIONAL, INC., *London*
PRENTICE-HALL OF AUSTRALIA, PTY. LTD., *Sydney*
PRENTICE-HALL OF CANADA, LTD., *Toronto*
PRENTICE-HALL OF INDIA PRIVATE LIMITED, *New Delhi*
PRENTICE-HALL OF JAPAN, INC., *Tokyo*

781.42
B534e

Preface

This collection is intended, while presenting a body of music of high intrinsic value, to illustrate the techniques of eighteenth-century counterpoint. Too often the study of Baroque counterpoint has had, for illustration and analysis, to make use of limited selections of published scores, usually restricted to a few keyboard works of J. S. Bach and Handel. An assemblage of a broad range of music for this purpose, published in a single volume, constitutes a resource which we hope will prove of stimulating content, diversity, and practical value.

We have sought to put together an anthology of considerable scope. Incorporating works of the later seventeenth and the first half of the eighteenth centuries, the collection also contains examples from those literatures of the late eighteenth and early nineteenth centuries which illustrate the survival of Baroque contrapuntal practices. The volume includes choral, orchestral, and chamber music in addition to a necessary majority of keyboard works. Inevitably, Bach and Handel are the composers most extensively represented. Some of the selections are of considerable textural and structural complexity, but many are two-voice works accessible at the earliest stages of contrapuntal study.

A listing of our sources, as well as a classification by page number, showing reference to examples as to medium, form, and number of voices, is included. The music is organized chronologically within each part, according to the composers' dates of birth, and in alphabetical sequence within the space given to each composer.

The medium of performance is not indicated for numerous works of J. S. Bach commonly assumed to have been written for harpsichord or clavichord, or for excerpts from Bach's *Art of the Fugue* and *Musical Offering*, whose instrumentation the composer did not specify.

Except for occasional matters of editorial or practical interest, the collection is without annotation and its adaptation to classroom and reference needs is left to be determined by particular circumstances.

We have not attempted to take up in any depth the complex question of the execution of ornaments. A useful, brief, and authoritative reference, based on contemporaneous sources (especially K. P. E. Bach, Quantz, F. Couperin, and Marpurg) is the Preface to Ralph Kirkpatrick's edition of Bach's *Goldberg Variations* (New York: G. Schirmer, Inc., 1938).

A few examples have been taken from copyrighted editions, and we are indebted to the various publishers and copyright owners whose permission is acknowledged where these examples occur. The encouragement and assistance of our colleagues, Dr. Hans T. David and Dr. Ellwood Derr, must be gratefully mentioned; both brought specific examples to our attention and generously gave time to the discussion of questions we raised.

At the same time, we wish to make explicit our exclusive responsibility for the organization of this volume, and for decisions of editorial policy.

W. B.
E. C.

Contents

PART TWO

Johann Sebastian Bach (1685-1750)

PART THREE

Georg Frideric Handel (1685-1759)

PART FOUR

The Late Eighteenth Century

Wilhelm Friedemann Bach (1710-1784)

PART FIVE

The Early Nineteenth Century

PART ONE

Predecessors and Contemporaries of Bach

Johann Kaspar Kerll (1627-1693)

RICERCAR ON D*

for organ

*Adolf Sandberger, ed., *Johann Kaspar Kerll Ausgewählte Werke* in *Denkmäler der Tonkunst in Bayern* (Leipzig: Breitkopf & Härtel, 1900-38), II(ii), pp. 59-60. Reprinted by permission.

3

4

Dietrich Buxtehude (1637-1707)

FUGUE IN G*

for organ

*Max Seiffert, ed., *Dietrich Buxtehude Orgelwerke: Freie Kompositionen* (Wiesbaden: Breitkopf & Härtel, 1952), II, pp. 125-126. Reprinted by permission.

Dietrich Buxtehude

ORGAN CHORALES

Erhalt uns Herr bei deinem Wort (Motet)*

*Hermann Keller, ed., *Dietrich Buxtehude: Ausgewählte Choralbearbeitungen* (C. F. Peters Corporation, New York, N. Y. 10016, 1939), pp. 12-13. Reprinted by permission. The text of the chorale, included in the Peters edition, has been deleted.

Jesu Christus, unser Heiland*

*Hermann Keller, ed., *Dietrich Buxtehude: Ausgewählte Choralbearbeitungen* (C. F. Peters Corporation, New York, N.Y. 10016, 1939), p. 26. Reprinted by permission. The text of the chorale, included in the Peters edition, has been deleted.

Johann Christoph Bach (1642-1703)

PRELUDE AND FUGUE IN E-FLAT

for organ

Fugue

Johann Krieger (1651-1735)

RICERCAR ON A*

for organ

*Max Seiffert, ed., *Johann Krieger Anmuthige Clavier-Übung* in *Denkmäler der Tonkunst in Bayern* (Leipzig: Breitkopf & Härtel, 1900-38), XVIII, pp. 40-41. Reprinted by permission.

23

24

Johann Pachelbel (1653-1706)

MAGNIFICAT FUGUE NO. 15 ON D*

for organ

* Max Seiffert, ed., *Organum* (Cologne: Fr. Kistner & C. F. W. Siegel & Co.), Ser. 4, No. 14, pp. 16-17. Reprinted by permission.

Arcangelo Corelli (1653-1713)

SONATA IN B MINOR, OP. 1, NO. 6

(second movement)

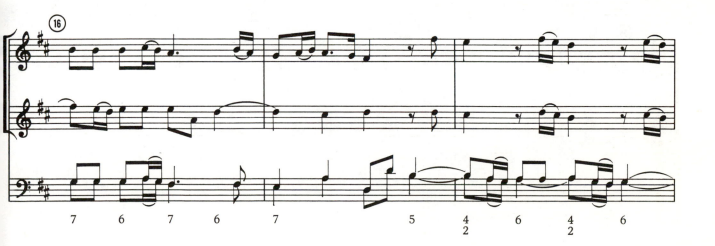

Arcangelo Corelli

SONATA IN F, OP. 3, NO. 1

(second movement)

Henry Purcell (c. 1659-1695)

*GLORIA PATRI**

*4 in 2 *Arsin per Thesin*.

Anthony Lewis and Nigel Fortune, eds., *The Works of Henry Purcell* (London: Novello and Co., Ltd., 1962), XXXII, pp. 161-162. Reprinted by permission of The H. W. Gray Co., Inc. An organ accompaniment included in the Novello edition has been deleted.

Henry Purcell
SUITE NO. 3 IN G
for harpsichord

Prelude*

*Execution of ornaments: = ; = a trill (shake) starting from the upper note. The contemporaneous *Rules for Graces* quoted in our source (q.v.) says of the shake that if it be on "a note with a point to it you are to hold all the note plain and shake only the point." Thus, the execution at m. 25 would be or , depending on whether "all the note plain" refers to the principal note or the auxiliary (backfall). (See also the edition by Howard Ferguson, published by Stainer and Bell, London, 1964).

**Ferguson gives .

38

40

Alessandro Scarlatti (1660-1725)

SONATA IN G MINOR

(first movement)*

*Hans T. David, ed., *Alessandro Scarlatti: Sonata a quattro in G Minor* (New York: The New York Public Library, 1938). Reprinted by permission.

Georg Böhm (1661-1733)

ORGAN CHORALES

Christ lag in Todesbanden (Motet)*

*Gesa Wolgast, ed., *Georg Böhm Sämtliche Werke: Klavier-und Orgelwerke* (Wiesbaden: Breitkopf & Härtel, 1952) II, pp. 102-103. Reprinted by permission.

Vom Himmel hoch da komm ich her (Motet)*

*Gesa Wolgast, ed., *Georg Böhm Sämtliche Werke: Klavier-und Orgelwerke* (Wiesbaden: Breitkopf & Härtel, 1952) II, pp. 141-142. Reprinted by permission.

Johann Kaspar Ferdinand Fischer (c. 1665-1746)

*ARIADNE MUSICA**

Preludes and Fugues

for organ

No. 3 in D minor

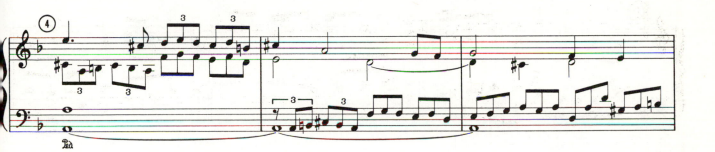

*Ernst Kaller, ed., *Liber Organi: Deutsche Meister des 16. und 17. Jahrhunderts* (Mainz: Schott's Söhne, 1935), II, pp. 6-7, 11, 14-15, 16-17. Reprinted by permission.

Fugue

No. 6 in E minor

Prelude

Fugue

No. 8 in E

Prelude

Fugue

No. 9 in F minor

Prelude

François Couperin (1668-1733)

MESSE POUR LES PAROISSES

for organ

Fugue in D minor*

*Fugue sur les jeux d'anches from *Messe pour les Paroisses,* Paul Brunold, ed. In *Oeuvres Complètes de François Couperin* (Paris: Éditions de l'Oiseau Lyre, 1932), VI, pp. 12-13. Reprinted by permission.

Georg Philipp Telemann (1681-1767)

SONATA IN E MINOR

for two flutes

(third movement)*

*G. Hausswald, ed., *G. P. Telemann: Musikalische Werke* (Kassel and Basel: Bärenreiter Verlag, 1955), VII, pp. 26-27. Reprinted by permission.

Gottlieb Muffat (1690-1770)

FUGUE IN G MINOR*

for organ

*Ernst Kaller, ed., *Liber Organi: Deutsche Meister des 16. und 17. Jahrhunderts* (Mainz: Schott's Söhne, 1935), I, pp. 38-40. Reprinted by permission. The organ registration is omitted and changes in the notation of voice-leading have been made by the present editors.

PART TWO

Johann Sebastian Bach

Johann Sebastian Bach (1685-1750)

ART OF THE FUGUE

Contrapunctus VIII (Triple Fugue)*

*Hans Gal, ed., *J. S. Bach: Die Kunst der Fuge* (London: Boosey and Hawkes, Ltd., 1951), pp. 32-38. Reprinted by permission.

80

82

Contrapunctus **X** (Double Fugue)*

*Hans Gal, ed., *J. S. Bach: Die Kunst der Fuge* (London: Boosey and Hawkes, Ltd., 1951), pp. 45-50. Reprinted by permission.

96

98

J. S. Bach

DUET IN F*

*From Clavier-Übung, Part III.

*Fermatas indicate conclusion of *da capo*:

or

100

Dal Segno

J. S. Bach
ENGLISH SUITE NO. 1 IN A

Gigue

J. S. Bach

ENGLISH SUITE NO. 5 IN E MINOR

Gigue

J. S. Bach

FRENCH SUITE NO. 3 IN B MINOR

Allemande

J. S. Bach

FUGUE IN C

for organ

114

115

117

118

119

J. S. Bach

FUGUE IN C MINOR

for organ

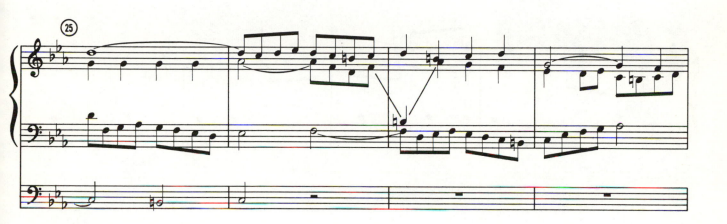

124

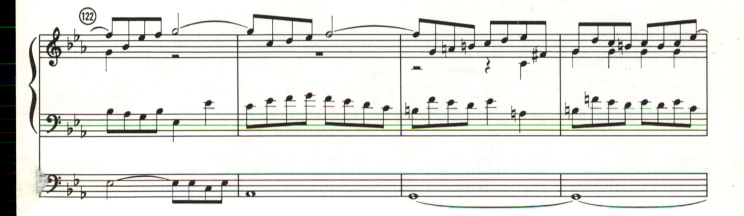

J. S. Bach

GOLDBERG VARIATIONS

Variation 15

Canon at the fifth in contrary motion
Andante

Variation 18

Canon at the sixth

J. S. Bach

INVENTIONS IN TWO VOICES

No. 1 in C*

*The numbering adopted here is that of the edition of the *Bach-Gesellschaft*.

No. 2 in C minor

No. 4 in D minor

No. 6 in E

No. 11 in G minor

No. 13 in A minor

J. S. Bach

INVENTIONS IN THREE VOICES*

No. 1 in C

*Originally titled *Sinfoniae*.

No. 3 in D

No. 7 in E minor

No. 8 in F

159

No. 9 in F minor

161

No. 14 in B-flat

J. S. Bach
MASS IN B MINOR
Kyrie eleison

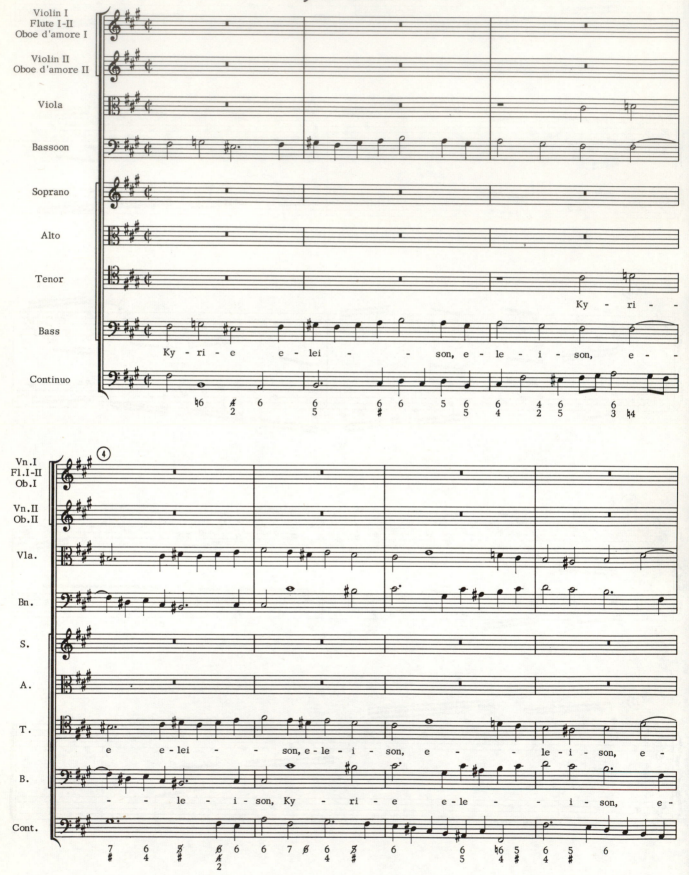

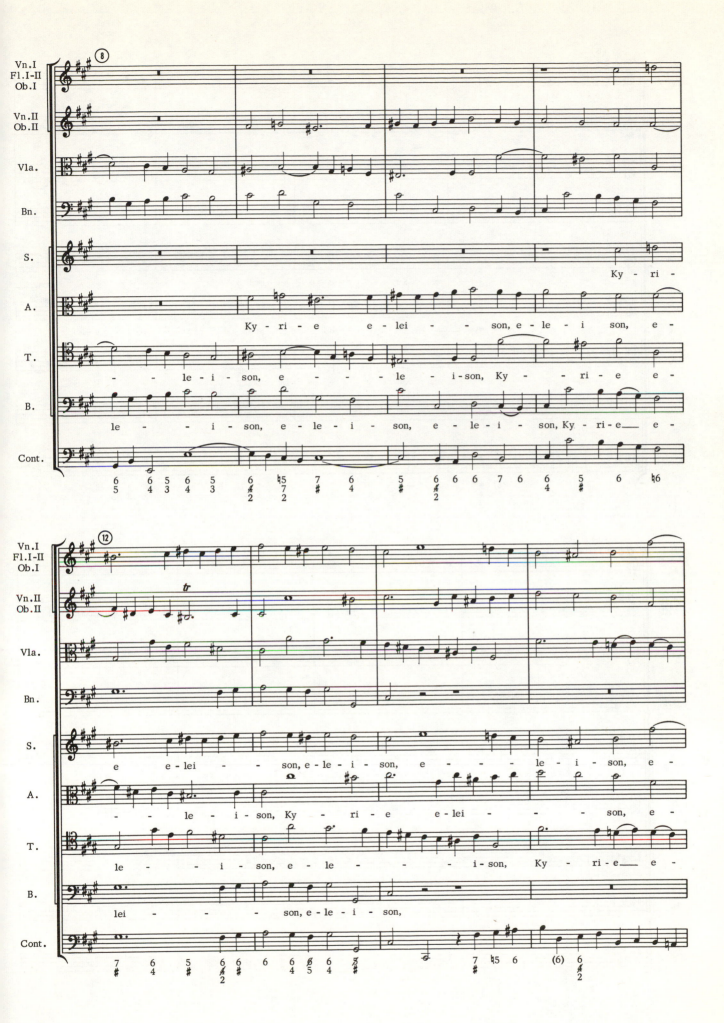

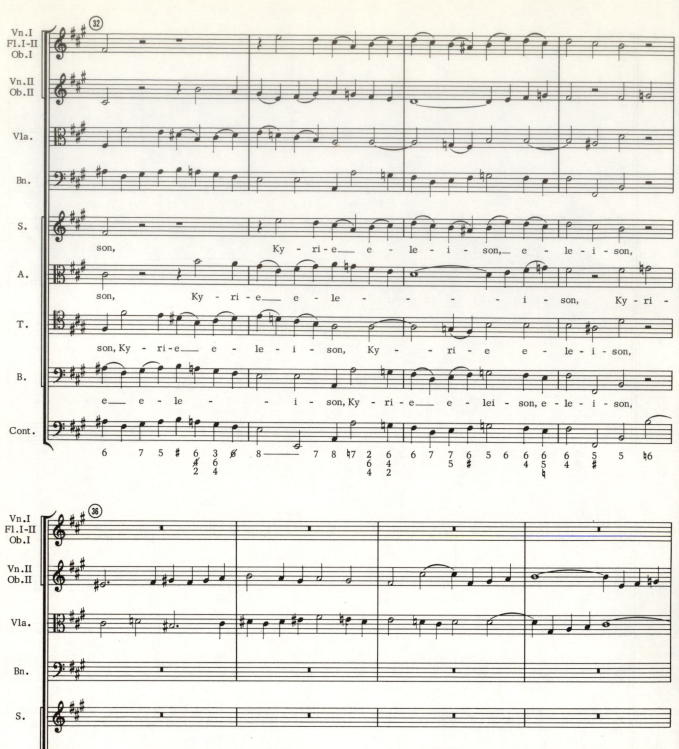

J. S. Bach
MASS IN B MINOR
Gratias agimus tibi

183

J. S. Bach?

MINUET IN A MINOR*

*From *Notebook for Anna Magdalena Bach.*

J. S. Bach

MUSICAL OFFERING

Eight Canons*

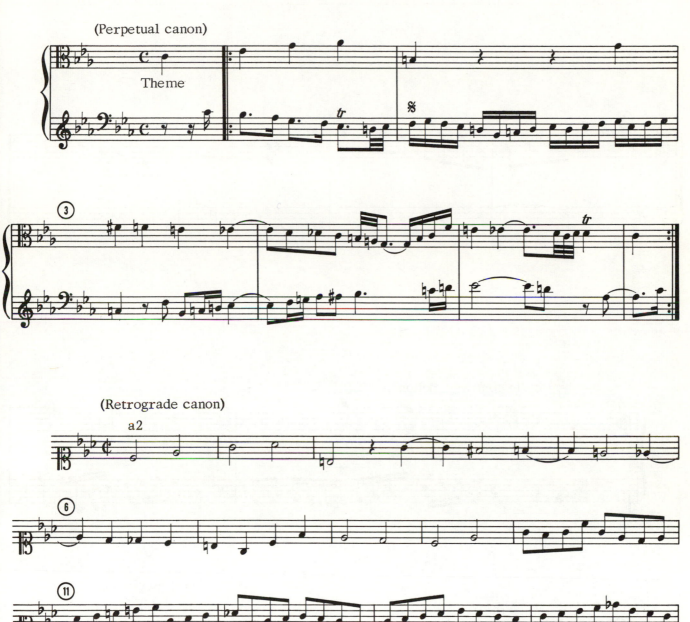

(Perpetual canon)

Theme

(Retrograde canon)

---

*For historical and practical annotations regarding the *Musical Offering,* and for solutions to the canons included here, the reader may wish to consult the edition by Hans T. David (New York: G. Schirmer, Inc., 1944) as well as Dr. David's book, *J. S. Bach's 'Musical Offering': History, Interpretation, and Analysis* (New York, G. Schirmer, Inc., 1945).

a2 (Violins at the unison)

Theme

a2 (In contrary motion)

Theme

190

a2 (In augmentation and in contrary motion)

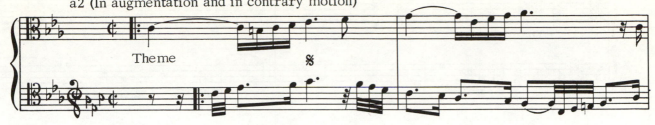

Theme

a2 (Spiral canon)

Theme

Canon a2

Quaerendo invenietis.*

*Seek and find.

Canon a4

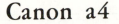

J. S. Bach

ORGAN CHORALES

Allein Gott in der Höh' sei Ehr' (Prelude)

196

197

Allein Gott in der Höh' sei Ehr' (Fugue)

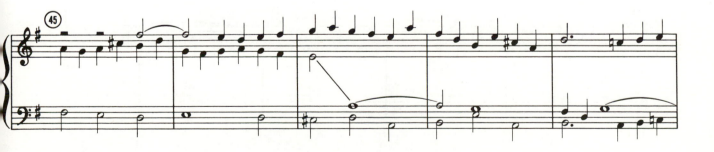

Allein Gott in der Höh' sei Ehr' (Fughetta)

Allein Gott in der Höh' sei Ehr' (Trio)

Aus tiefer Noth schrei' ich zu Dir (Motet)

Christ unser Herr zum Jordan kam (Invention)

Christus, der uns selig macht (Canon)

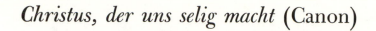

Jesu, meine Freude (Fantasy)

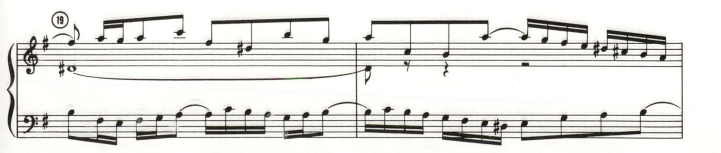

227

Nun komm' der Heiden Heiland

J. S. Bach

SINGET DEM HERRN EIN NEUES LIED (MOTET)

Alles, was Odem hat

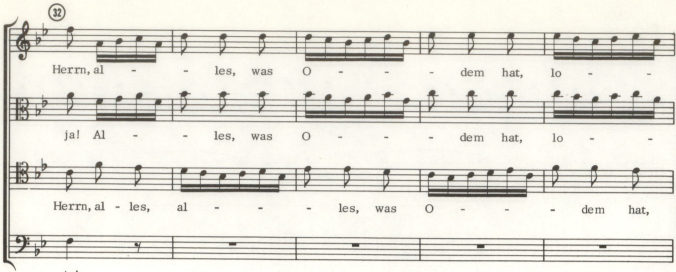

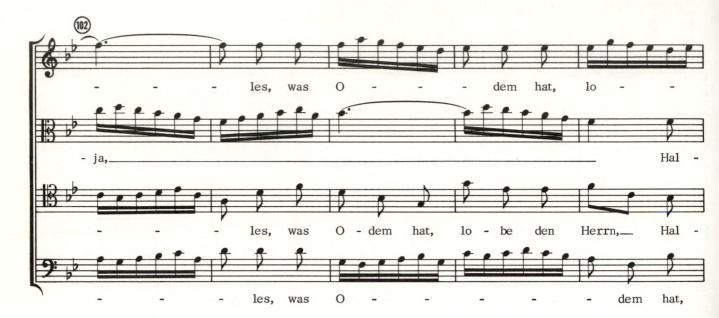

J. S. Bach

SONATA IN A MINOR

for violin alone

Fugue

241

243

J. S. Bach

WELL-TEMPERED CLAVIER, BOOK I

Fugue No. 1 in C

Fugue No. 2 in C minor

Fugue No. 6 in D minor

Fugue No. 8 in D-sharp minor

Fugue No. 10 in E minor

Fugue No. 16 in G minor

Fugue No. 22 in B-flat minor

J. S. Bach

WELL-TEMPERED CLAVIER, BOOK II

Prelude No. 2 in C minor

Fugue No. 2 in C minor

or:

Fugue No. 5 in D

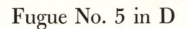

Fugue No. 17 in A-flat

Prelude No. 20 in A minor

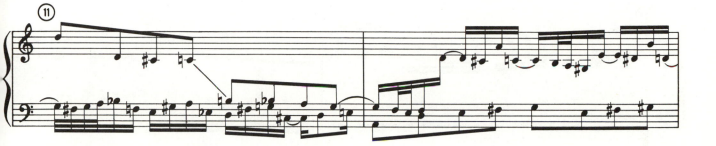

or:

Fugue No. 20 in A minor

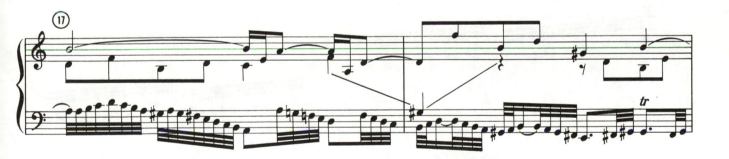

PART THREE

Georg Frideric Handel

Georg Frideric Handel (1685-1759)

CONCERTO GROSSO IN F, OP. 6, NO. 9

(fourth movement)

*Concertino and ripieno.

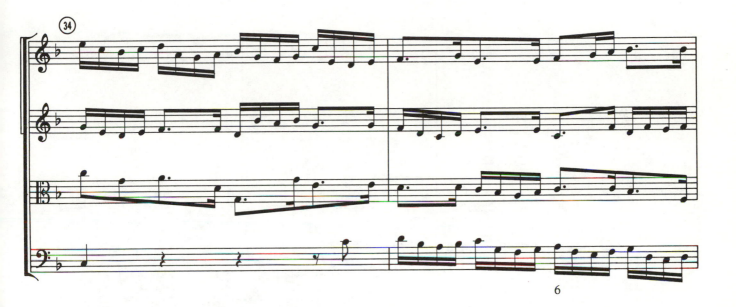

G. F. Handel

FUGUE IN A MINOR

for harpsichord

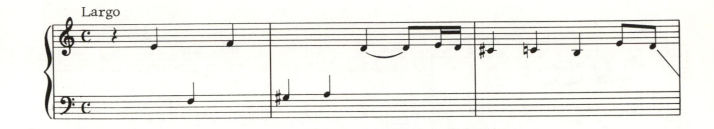

*As in similar instances following, the upper voices appear to cross.

G. F. Handel
FUGUE IN C MINOR

for harpsichord

G. F. Handel

JUDAS MACCABEUS

To our great God

*Most of the figures under the bass line are editorial additions.

J. S. Bach

WELL-TEMPERED CLAVIER, BOOK I

Fugue No. 1 in C

Fugue No. 2 in C minor

Fugue No. 6 in D minor

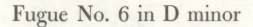

Fugue No. 8 in D-sharp minor

257

Fugue No. 10 in E minor

Fugue No. 16 in G minor

Fugue No. 22 in B-flat minor

J. S. Bach

WELL-TEMPERED CLAVIER, BOOK II

Prelude No. 2 in C minor

Fugue No. 2 in C minor

or:

Fugue No. 5 in D

al rovescio

al rovescio

al rovescio

al rovescio

Wolfgang Amadeus Mozart (1756-1791)

CANON: *SELIG, SELIG ALLE*,* K. 230

for two voices

*On Hölty's *Elegie beim Grabe meines Vaters* (Elegy at the Grave of my Father).

al-le, al - le, se-lig, se-lig sie, die im Herrn ent-

Se - lig,_ se - lig al - le, se-lig, se-lig sie,

- schlie-fen! Auch se - lig, se-lig, Freund, bist du. En - gel brach-ten dir den Kranz,

die im Herrn ent-schlie - fen! Auch se - lig, se-lig, Freund bist du. En-gel

und die En - gel rie - fen, und du gingst in Got-tes_

brach-ten dir den Kranz, und die En - gel rie - fen, und du

Ruh, und du gingst zur Ruh. Ja, se - lig_ Ruh.

gingst in Got-tes_ Ruh, und du gingst zur Ruh. du gingst zur Ruh.

W. A. Mozart

FANTASY AND FUGUE IN C, K. 394

for piano

Fugue

Andante maestoso

W. A. Mozart

REQUIEM MASS, K. 626

Kyrie eleison

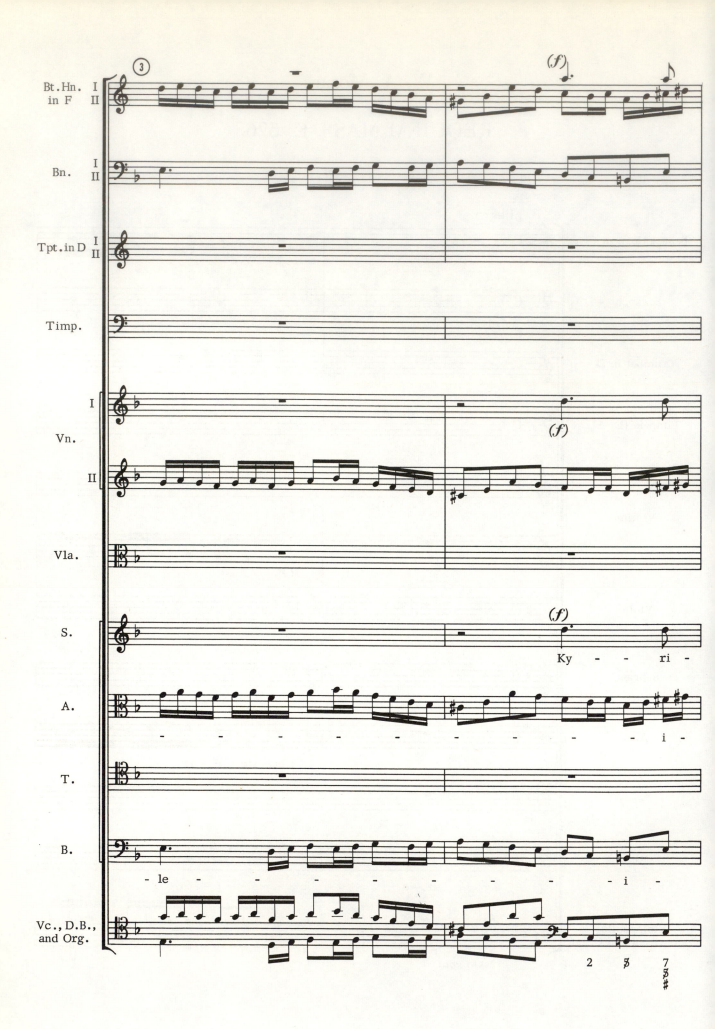

*Mozart's use of the tenor clef at this and subsequent points is often interpreted to indicate that the cellos play without the basses, the latter re-entering with the resumption of the bass voice.

375

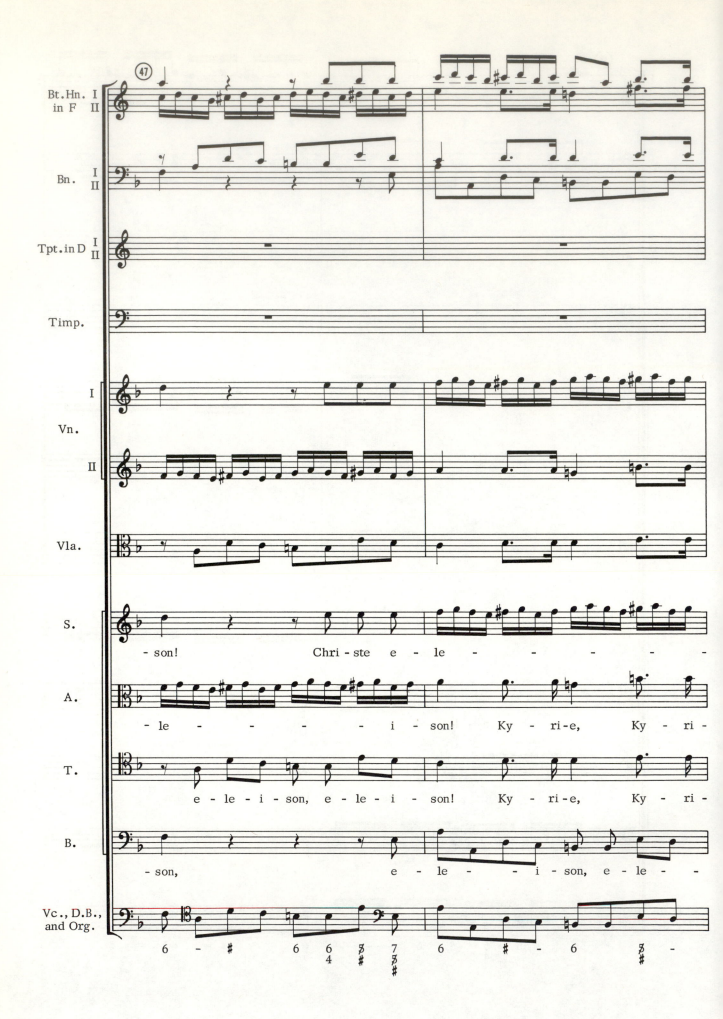

PART FIVE

The Early Nineteenth Century

Ludwig van Beethoven (1770-1827)

FUGUE IN D, OP. 137

for string quintet

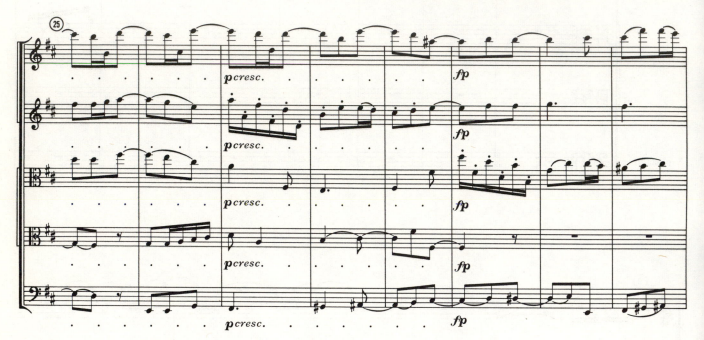

Felix Mendelssohn (1809-1847)

SIX PRELUDES AND FUGUES, OP. 35

for piano

Fugue No. 3 in B minor

Allegro con brio

Robert Schumann (1810-1856)

SIX FUGUES ON THE NAME OF BACH, OP. 60

for organ

Fugue No. 3 in G minor

Sources

Bach, Johann Christoph. *Prelude and Fugue in E-flat for Organ.* In Ritter, A. G., *Zur Geschichte des Orgelspiels,* Vol. II. Leipzig: Max Hesse's Verlag, 1884.

Bach, Johann Sebastian. *Die Kunst der Fuge,* ed. Hans Gal. London: Boosey & Hawkes, Ltd., 1951.

Bach, Johann Sebastian. *Johann Sebastian Bach's Werke.* Leipzig: Bach Gesellschaft, 1851-1900. Vols. III, VI, XIII, XIV XV, XXV, XXVII, XXXI, XXXIX, XL, and XLIII(ii).

Bach, Karl Philipp Emanuel. *Zwei Duos,* ed. Wolfgang Stephan. In *Nagels Musik-Archiv,* No. 35. London: Schott & Co., 1928.

Bach, Wilhelm Friedemann. *Sämtliche Klaviersonaten,* ed. Friedrich Blume. In *Nagels Musik-Archiv,* No. 156. Kassel and Basel: Bärenreiter-Verlag, 1959.

Bach, Wilhelm Friedemann. *Zwei Sonaten für zwei Querflöten allein,* ed. Albert Rodemann. In *Nagels Musik-Archiv,* No. 120. Kassel and Basel: Bärenreiter-Verlag, 1960.

Beethoven, Ludwig van. *Ludwig van Beethoven's Werke.* Leipzig: Breitkopf & Härtel, 1864-67. Series 5.

Böhm, Georg. *Sämtliche Werke: Klavier- und Orgelwerke,* ed. Gesa Wolgast. Wiesbaden: Breitkopf & Härtel, 1952. Vol. II.

Buxtehude, Dietrich. *Ausgewählte Choralbearbeitungen,* ed. Hermann Keller. Leipzig: C. F. Peters, 1939.

Buxtehude, Dietrich. *Dietrich Buxtehude Orgelwerke: Freie Kompositionen,* ed. Max Seiffert. Wiesbaden: Breitkopf & Härtel, 1952. Vol. II.

Corelli, Arcangelo. *Les Oeuvres de Arcangelo Corelli,* ed. Fr. Chrysander. London: Augener & Co., 1890. Vols. I and II.

Couperin, François. *Pièces d'orgue consistantes en deux messes,* ed. Paul Brunold. In *Oeuvres complètes de François Couperin,* VI. Paris: Editions de l'Oiseau Lyre, 1932.

Fischer, Johann Kaspar Ferdinand. *Ariadne Musica,* ed. Ernst Kaller. In *Liber Organi: Deutsche Meister des 16. und 17. Jahrhunderts,* Vol. II. Mainz: B. Schott's Söhne, 1935.

Handel, Georg Frideric. *George Friedrich Händel's Werke,* ed. Fr. Chrysander. Leipzig: Händel Gesellschaft, 1856-94. Vols. II, XXII, XXVII, and XXX.

Haydn, Franz Joseph. *String Quartet, Op. 20, No. 6*. London-Zurich: Ernst Eulenberg Ltd.

Kerll, Johann Kaspar. *Ausgewählte Werke*, ed. Adolf Sandberger. In *Denkmäler der Tonkunst in Bayern*, Vol. II(ii). Leipzig: Breitkopf & Härtel, 1900-38.

Krieger, Johann. *Anmuthige Clavier-Übung*, ed. Max Seiffert. In *Denkmäler der Tonkunst in Bayern*, Vol. XVIII. Leipzig: Breitkopf & Härtel, 1900-38.

Mendelssohn, Felix. *Felix Mendelssohn Bartholdy's Werke*, ed. Julius Rietz. Leipzig: Breitkopf & Härtel, 1874-77. Series 11, Vol. II.

Mozart, Wolfgang Amadeus. *W. A. Mozart's Werke*. Leipzig: Breitkopf & Härtel, 1876-86. Series 7(2), 20, and 24.

Muffat, Gottlieb. *Fuge in G moll*, ed. Ernst Kaller. In *Liber Organi: Deutsche Meister des 16. und 17. Jahrhunderts*, Vol. I. Mainz: B. Schott's Söhne, 1935.

Pachelbel, Johann. *94 Compositionen zumeist Fugen über das Magnificat*, ed. Hugo Botstiber and Max Seiffert. In *Denkmäler der Tonkunst in Österreich*, Vol. VIII(ii). Vienna: Artaria and Company, 1894- .

Purcell, Henry. *The Works of Henry Purcell*. London: Novello & Co., 1878- . Vols. VI and XXXII.

Scarlatti, Alessandro. *Sonata a quattro in G minor*, ed. Hans T. David. New York: The New York Public Library, 1938.

Schumann, Robert. *Robert Schumann's Werke*, ed. Clara Schumann. Leipzig: Breitkopf & Härtel, 1886-93. Series 8.

Telemann, Georg Philipp. *Musikalische Werke*, ed. Günter Hausswald. Kassel and Basel: Bärenreiter-Verlag, 1955. Vol. VII.

Classification of Examples

I. *Medium of performance*

Chamber ensemble, 28, 32, 41, 64, 323, 331, 334, 336, 383

Chorus and orchestra, 166, 174, 308, 355

Keyboard other than organ, 38, 99, 104, 106, 110, 132, 134, 136, 138, 141, 143, 145, 148, 151, 153, 156, 158, 161, 163, 188, 247, 250, 252, 254, 261, 263, 267, 270, 273, 275, 279, 284, 288, 299, 304, 315, 320, 322, 329, 349, 387

Orchestra, 293

Organ, 3, 6, 10, 14, 16, 22, 25, 47, 51, 53, 55, 56, 59, 61, 67, 113, 121, 194, 198, 202, 204, 216, 219, 221, 224, 231, 396

Violin alone, 239

Voices, 36, 232, 347

II. *Number of voices*

Two voices, 38, 64, 99, 104, 110, 136, 138, 141, 143, 145, 148, 188, 189, 192, 261, 270, 284, 329, 331, 334, 347

Three voices, 6, 14, 28, 32, 73, 106, 132, 134, 151, 153, 156, 158, 161, 163, 189, 191, 194, 198, 202, 204, 219, 250, 252, 254, 288, 315, 322, 323, 349

Four voices, 3, 10, 16, 22, 25, 36, 41, 47, 51, 53, 55, 56, 59, 61, 89, 121, 193, 216, 221, 232, 247, 263, 273, 275, 279, 293, 304, 336, 355

Five voices, 231, 267, 383, 396

Variable number of voices, 67 (3-4), 113 (4-5), 166 (4-5), 174, 224 (3-4), 239, 299 (3-4), 308, 320 (2-3), 387

III. *Form or genre*

Canon, 30, 132, 134, 189, 190, 192, 221, 329, 347

Dance, 104, 106, 110, 188, 320, 322, 329

Fugue (or ricercar), 3, 6, 18, 22, 25, 28, 41, 53, 55, 56, 59, 61, 67, 73, 89, 99, 113, 121, 166, 198, 202, 232, 239, 247, 250, 252, 254, 261, 263, 267, 273, 275, 279, 288, 293, 299, 304, 308, 315, 323, 336, 349, 355, 383, 387, 396

Invention, 64, 99, 136, 138, 141, 143, 145, 148, 151, 153, 156, 158, 161, 163, 219, 331

Organ chorale, 10, 14, 47, 51, 194, 198, 202, 204, 216, 219, 221, 224, 231

Prelude, 16, 38, 53, 55, 56, 59, 270, 284